THE LITTLE BOOK OF CHEESE TIPS

ANDREW LANGLEY

THE LITTLE BOOK OF
CHEESE
TIPS

ANDREW LANGLEY

Absolute Press

First published in Great Britain in 2005 by
Absolute Press
Scarborough House, 29 James Street West
Bath BA1 2BT, England
Phone 44 (0) 1225 316013 **Fax** 44 (0) 1225 445836
E-mail info@absolutepress.co.uk
Web www.absolutepress.co.uk

A catalogue record of this book is available
from the British Library

ISBN 1 904573 30 4

Printed and bound in Italy by Legoprint

'A dessert without cheese is like a beautiful woman who is missing an eye.'

Jean-Anthelme Brillat-Savarin

Always buy your cheese from a specialist shop

where you can see it being cut.
Pre-cut portions may have hung around for
days, and the exposed surfaces quickly gain
rancid flavours. Plastic wrapping doesn't help.

Buy grating cheeses such as Parmesan **in a block,** instead of ready-grated. Grated cheese has a huge surface area, and will have lost most of its aroma and freshness, even if it is sealed in a packet.

The easiest way to mix cheese into a sauce

or a dish is grate it as finely and spread it as widely as possible. This way, it's less likely to go lumpy.

Take your time when melting cheese. Put it over a low heat and be patient, or else it may get tough and leathery. Worse still, it may start separating into its constituent oils and liquids.

Take the cheese out of the fridge at least two hours before you serve it. This allows time for the milk fats to soften up and release the flavours. It will also give the cheese a softer texture.

Camembert and other **soft cheeses need time to ripen.**

This won't happen in a fridge, which will be too cold to let nature take its course. So leave the cheese somewhere at room temperature (though not too warm).

Don't worry if you very occasionally find

something crunchy in your cheese. These will probably

be salty crystals , a natural part of the ripening
process. Crystals occur in many kinds of
cheese, from Parmesan and Cheddar to
Roquefort and Gouda.

Little and often.

These are two of the

key words when cheese-buying.

Unless you're entertaining, small portions are enough. You'll eat them within a couple of days and they will stay fresh. Then go out and buy a little more.

When choosing cheese in a shop, first of all
use your eyes.
Avoid anything which has beads of moisture
or fat on it. This probably means that it has been
kept at too high a temperature.

When choosing cheese be sure to
use your nose.
Be bold and give the cheese a good hard sniff.
If you can smell a lot of ammonia, it may
be over-ripe. Unless you're going to eat it
straightaway and love very strong tastes,
don't buy it.

The best sort of cheese knife

is one with large cut-outs in the blade.
This prevents you from squashing soft cheeses
as you press down on them. The knife should
also have a serrated edge, and prongs to pick
up the cut pieces.

What is the best (and politest) way to cut cheese from a wedge? The age-old answer is:

leave it in the same shape as you found it.

This means slicing neatly from rind to tip, and getting an even quantity of outside and middle.

13

Should the cheese be served
before or after
dessert? In France and
other parts of Europe it arrives before dessert,
so that diners can go on drinking a red wine.
In Britain and the USA cheese is often served
at the end of a meal.

A cheese slicer is traditionally used

to cut whole rounds of cheese such as Stilton.

Draw the blade (which is at right angles to the handle) gently towards you, scraping a thin slice from the top of the cheese.

Cheesy crisps go perfectly with
a pre-dinner glass of wine or sherry. Grate some

mature Cheddar or Gruyere and place on a non-stick baking sheet in little mounds about 3 inches (6cm) across. Bake at a fairly high heat for ten minutes, then cool on a wire rack.

The simplest starter for any meal

consists of two delicious ingredients – a slice of good quality Pecorino and a ripe, juicy pear. Nothing else... except maybe a glass of white wine.

Use up
all those
odds and ends

by making potted cheese. In a processor,
simply whizz together 1 lb (450g) of cheese
leftovers (the tastier the better) with 4oz (100g)
of butter, a glass of sherry and pinches of
mustard and nutmeg. Pack in little jars and
seal with clarified butter.

Make your own cottage cheese.

Warm 2 pints (1 litre) of milk to blood heat, then stir in a rennet tablet (the ones used to make junket). After two hours in a warm place, slice the curd into cubes and heat it all very gently again. Place the lot in a muslin bag and drain for three hours or more. Add a little salt.

Planning a hearty Boxing Day walk?

Keep out the cold with a chunk of Cheshire cheese and a slice of Christmas cake – one of those heavenly combinations of taste and texture!

20

Manchego, the hard ewes' milk cheese from Spain, makes **a brilliant cheese fritter.** Whisk two egg whites into peaks, mix in 4 oz (100g) of grated Manchego, plus breadcrumbs, thyme and sweet smoked paprika. Deep-fry little balls of the mixture gently in olive oil.

A beef fillet **steak** can be very tender but very bland. **Give it some oomph** with a Rocquefort and horseradish topping. Mix together Rocquefort, creamed horseradish and large-leaf parsley in a processor. Place on top of the seared steaks and pop under the grill for a couple of minutes.

When you're making a

pizza topped with Mozzarella,

prepare the cheese thirty minutes ahead.
Grate the Mozzarella into a bowl, mix in a little
olive oil and ground black pepper and let stand.
This gives an extra dimension to the taste.

23

Membrillo is the Spanish term for quince 'cheese' – though it's not really cheese at all. However, a little cube on a piece of Manchego makes

a superb tapas dish

– along with a glass of oloroso sherry.

It's best to **lay out your cheese board** at least an hour before a meal. It's even better to protect the cheese under a glass or china dome. Pop a cube or two of sugar under the dome, as this will absorb the moisture given out by the cheese.

When storing a ripening or runny cheese

such as Brie, wrap the cut edge tightly in cling film, or place against a strip of cardboard. This will stop it from oozing out and losing taste and texture.

Some soft cheeses, such as Livarot and Munster, are famous (and feared) for their **pungent smell and seriously strong taste.**

Serve them with sweet, hard fruit such as pears and apples to make a soothing contrast.

The classic cheese fondue

has three absolutely essential ingredients –
Gruyére, kirsch and a good Riesling wine.
Rub the pot with a garlic clove, then heat grated
cheese (100 g or 4oz) and wine (half a glass)
slowly, stirring all the time. Mix 2 tablespoons
of kirsch with a tablespoon of cornflour, then
stir this into the pot, adding butter. Start dipping
your bread into the fondue straightaway.

28

A poor man's fondue

can be made with cheese leftovers. Grate the cheese and heat gently with white wine, garlic, mustard and seasoning. When it's thick, add two or three well-beaten eggs and keep stirring. Eat at once

Barbecued bananas (in their skins) are delicious enough on their own, but they enter a new dimension when served with Mascarpone.

Mix a tub of Mascarpone with a slug of rum, a big spoonful of sugar

and a pinch of cinnamon. Split open the grilled bananas and spread the mixture over.

Haloumi is a rubbery sort of cheese from Greece which **cries out to be grilled.** Cook slices under the grill for four minutes each side, then serve with a green salad dressed with lemon juice and olive oil.

Some taste combinations are made in heaven.
Try combining **Pecorino, chopped pear** and mashed (cooked) **broad beans on toast.** A drop of sherry vinegar and a slosh of olive oil completes the **magic.**

Give your cheeses room on the board.

When presenting a board of cheese, limit the choice to four or five. A larger number will crowd together, producing a confusing jumble of aromas and tastes.

Cheese is the original fast food. For a
speedy snack,
toast slices of sourdough bread, brush with oil
(and a little white wine, if you've got a bottle
open) and cover with slivers of Gruyére or
crumbs of goat's cheese. Pop under the grill
for two minutes – then eat.

Butter can be served with cheese

– as long as it is unsalted.
Butter spread on bread makes a suitable surface
for bits of crumbly cheese to stick to.
Some people also like butter because it
stops runny cheeses sinking into the bread.

35

Split a fresh bagel and pull out the soft bread inside.

Then fill the shells with a layer of cream cheese, lightly salted, a sprinkling of dill and slices of smoked salmon. Add a drop of lemon juice, a pinch of cayenne, and you're away.

Ever grilled a goat's cheese?

If you have then try this slightly more sophisticated version. Wrap a slice of prosciutto round a small round goat's cheese (such as Crottin), and grill on both sides. Mash some black olives and spread on a slice of toast. Put the cheese on top.

37

The cheese should always be
the star of the cheese board.
Even so, a few subtle decorations around
the cheese will enhance its appearance.
Try leaves – vine, hay, even nasturtium;
or fruits – grapes, tangerines or cherry tomatoes.

Crumbly Caerphilly

can be turned into herby

Glamorgan sausages.

Mix with equal quantities of breadcrumbs and chopped leeks, plus an egg yolk and seasoning. Roll into sausage shapes, cover in beaten egg and more breadcrumbs, and fry in butter.

Aligot is **a classic cheesy dish** from the Auvergne. Put boiled and mashed potato in a pan over low heat, and beat in butter, cream and milk. Now add chopped garlic and thin slices of young, fresh Cantal (the authentic ingredient), or Wensleydale. Keep stirring until you have a smooth pureé.

A true
Welsh rarebit

contains little that is really Welsh. Heat butter and a tablespoon of flour, then add about half a pint of beer and milk mixed. When it is boiling, fold in 4oz (110g) of grated Cheshire cheese and a teaspoon of mustard. Serve on slices of toast.

When you're melting cheeses into soups

and sauces, **remember to cut off the rind first.**

Rinds – even on soft cheeses like Brie – tend to stay hard and unmelted.

Cheese contains much less lactose than whole milk. Most of the lactose (a form of milk sugar) is contained by the liquid whey, which is removed in the cheese-making process. This is good news for for people who have

a low tolerance for lactose.

43

Turn Reblochon into

the easiest and most delicious of all cheese pies.

Simply sprinkle a whole Reblochon with pepper and thyme, then wrap it in rolled puff pastry. Brush with beaten egg and pop in a hottish oven for ten minutes. Eat without delay.

Labneh is **a soft yoghurt cheese from the Middle East** – and it's simple to make. Mix a jar of Greek yoghurt with a teaspoon of salt. Spoon it into a square of muslin and hang up to drain overnight over a bowl. Labneh mixed with fennel seeds or sage is brilliant for stuffing chicken breasts.

Blue cheese and honey is

a surprising but magical combination.

Take a slice of good cheese such as Maytag, Cashel Blue or Danish Blue, and drizzle a little runny honey all over.

Little round
goat cheeses
can be **transformed**
by marinating them in oil, Put thyme and sage leaves into a glass jar, then as many cheeses as will fit, separated by a sprinkling of more herbs (plus juniper berries). Pop a sprig of rosemary on top, and fill up the jar with olive oil. They will last for months.

Cheese and bread go together in almost any style.

An unusual combination is Feta and Mint Bread.

Knead two tablespoons of dried mint into an olive oil dough, then flatten it out and plonk 8oz (225g) of crumbled feta in the middle. Roll up and seal. Prove for an hour and bake for 40 minutes.

48

Today's **Stilton cheeses need no special treatment.** In the old days, people soused their Stiltons with port, in order to kill off the maggots which often throve inside the rind. Modern hygienic production and storage have made this unnecessary.

Transform lamb chops

with a Parmesan coating. Roll the chops in seasoned flour, then dip in beaten egg. Now roll again, this time in a mixture of grated Parmesan, sesame seeds and breadcrumbs. Roast in a hot oven for about twenty minutes.

Which wine goes best with cheese?

This varies, depending on the cheese. Strong cheese will swamp a fine red wine, so drink a robust Rioja, for example. Mild cheeses go well with lighter reds such as a Beaujolais, or even a delicate white such as a Vouvray. In general, though, try to match cheese with wine from the same locality.

Andrew Langley

Andrew Langley is a knowledgeable food and drink writer. Among his formative influences he lists a season picking grapes in Bordeaux, several years of raising sheep and chickens in Wiltshire and two decades drinking his grandmother's tea. He has written books on a number of Scottish and Irish whisky distilleries and is the editor of the highly regarded anthology of the writings of the legendary Victorian chef Alexis Soyer.

Little Tips from
Absolute Press

Also by Andrew Langley
The Little Book of Tea Tips (2.99)
The Little Book of Coffee Tips (2.99)
The Little Book of Wine Tips (2.99)

By Richard Maggs
The Little Book of Aga Tips (2.99)
The Little Book of Aga Tips 2 (2.99)
The Little Book of Aga Tips 3 (2.99)
The Little Book of Christmas Aga Tips (2.99)
The Little Book of Rayburn Tips (2.99)

All titles are available to order.
Cheques (made payable to Absolute Press)
or VISA/Mastercard details should be sent to:

Absolute Press
Scarborough House, 29 James Street West, Bath BA1 2BT.
Phone 01225 316 013 for any further details.

0 1 1 6 5 7
2 5 7
0 3 4 9.